Poems in the voice of Philip Seymou̶r̶ ̶
imagined people. Poems in the voice ̶
Seymour Hoffman adopting the personae of real and imagined people. Poems in the
voice of Marc McKee adopting the persona of a Marc McKee-like speaker adopting
the persona of Philip Seymour Hoffman adopting the personae of real and imagined
people. Poems in the mind of a reader imagining themselves invited into the mind
of Marc McKee adopting the persona of a Marc McKee-like speaker adopting the
persona of Philip Seymour Hoffman adopting the personae of real and imagined
people. Poems in the mind of a reader imagining themselves as some other reader
imagined by Marc McKee to be themselves imagining themselves invited into the
mind of Marc McKee adopting the persona of a Marc McKee-like speaker adopting
the persona of Philip Seymour Hoffman adopting the personae of real and imagined
people.
—Kathryn Nuernberger

Marc McKee's *Meta Meta Make-Belief* delivers his awareness of our awareness of the fic-
tions we tell ourselves, the ones we perhaps too reverently call 'memory' or 'history'
or 'biography.' McKee lays these out in their countless, little, linguistic pieces. His
poems are frenetic with nostalgia and reference, offering hints and glimpses into
this life and that one, but as in a Cubist painting, everything arrives in facets and
shards and all at once as if lyric confession itself is born of little more than the
mixed-up, gorgeous disaster of language: "I was a spark ferried by a catastrophe of
wind / then I was a little girl who loved the Beatles more // than dessert's inverted
chandeliers. / I pawed at the monster // slicking up the spooked conduit of my neck /
then stirred frantic, unwrecked, a little boy // in a little red incorrigible wagon..."
This is the part of the story where we realize these rich, playful poems might be ex-
actly right about language, living, and make-believing. For this, I am grateful to
have them.
—Jaswinder Bolina

In *Meta Meta Make-Belief,* Marc McKee reminds us "we're not dead yet" which is an im-
portant thing to be reminded of, because it means we can still do better, and we can
still make amends, still find what we>ve lost, or deal directly with what we've found.
In these poems, wired in series to show us a new movie of ourselves, Philip Seymour
Hoffman plays all of us playing Philip Seymour Hoffman, who's playing Marc
McKee, and as long as we're all playing—still talking and voicing over and acting and
improvising—the possibility for making believe and making belief means that we
can still draw pictures of each other's hearts, and those drawings can be the blue-
prints for "epic after epic after sorry fucking epic" and what could be better? What
could be more? In a world of so much worse, these poems soar! And then, more or
less safely, they bring us back to earth.
—Matt Hart

meta meta make-belief

poems

Marc McKee

Black
Lawrence
Press

Black
Lawrence
Press

www.blacklawrence.com

Executive Editor: Diane Goettel
Book and cover design: Amy Freels
Cover art: "TV Fun Squad" by Marc McKee

Published 2019 by Black Lawrence Press.
Printed in the United States.

To Camellia & Harry

Contents

make-belief

How Meta is This?: An Essay

Impossible to determine a singular *this*
that *how meta* "*is*." That 90s show about nothing
has a show within a show that starts to be
about nothing but has to be about something
and is terrible, making the show without
the within show victorious
and in the midst of that arc my father loses
his job, all our lives change, but that's real,
not *about* the real except there is no real
that isn't also *about* being real, cf. so many emcees,
hiya hip hop, personae personae personae
like to flip Ezra Pound's bones, so very
vampire slayer, the first episode of *BtVS* I see,
for example, pivotal season 4 finale,
a kind of vision/conspiracy board
that retroactively laces up what's come before
and prophesies what's to come only what's come
before are prophecies that didn't pan out,
failures in determinism that stay warnings
even now, *even now* one of the only things I like
about prophecies. There was that one song
by NOFX, remember NOFX? remember that song,
it was its own kind of essay, anything can be
an essay if you take the time to call it an essay
and did it ever get played on the radio?
Are there not like 1000 desperate, sloppy
9/11 metaphors masquerading
as hour-long serial melodramas
but then maybe 2 come correct, right, are
right, right? Write your guess on two postcards
and send one postcard to someone

you are sure will disagree with you
and one to one you are sure will not.
There's the scene in *Safety School*, not its
real name, where the fallen, above-it dick
with a terrified heart names a pencil, breaks it,
and the woman whose involuntary, audible reaction
is audible in a precisely performed way.
Two characters from that show have 30 seconds
at the end of most of the first three seasons
to pitch a diamond at us that chases
the pleasing fossil fuels of the other 21:30. So TV,
so all day, Tom Stoppard, but Shakespeare all day
every day, the part where the fool I am
mistakes the fool I am with Lear's, with Hamlet,
with Will his hack self hooting, cutting eyes, cutting
ayes to the penny rabble, one minute
he's romancing the break with the pretense
of the kingly body, then a snark follows hard upon
that rolls out like a carpet
down the whole mercy-forsaken plank we walk
then a dick joke / balls joke / vagina terror
joke but let's be clear: it is Philip Seymour Hoffman
in that one movie that I love just enough more
than all other fellow meta instants:
Can you see him there? Hospice nurse,
paging through soul-scurvying porno mag
classifieds. How on the phone he is.
How barely patient. How *for* his patient, so
This is a movie he says, not in so many words,
and in movies even when the sky rains
amphibious catharsis, even
when all the characters sing the same song
where some of my best friends just know
there should be an intermission instead
or a fire of napalm and petrol

that dials this movie back to "never happened"
even then, the most artificing
of an artificial thing lays out things true,
it is like the field dressing game of true things
happening. *This is a movie* he doesn't quite
say, but the movie says hey,
how about this movie, being a movie,
and Philip Seymour Hoffman never does anything
less than make you believe. Please pretend
you know this is a movie and act like it
because if that means to you anything like
what it means to me, you will help me
like I believe I would try to help you. Who
is even saying this. He wants you to believe
even art at its most absurd can lead you, propel you
into intervention, like "the lady blackmailer"
in another movie I love that you've almost certainly
never seen. Do we have all night, all we have
is night. Sometimes all we have is all the night
we have. Right. Allusion, Michael. Fake it till
etcetera. I have loved so many cartoons
reminding me they are cartoons, how they take
my hand. I once thought any move to meta
was a cheat. Just one bobble and meta
is meat. How meet. My son, 3 ½, says
we can read this book just skip the dragon.
I say I won't skip the dragon, but
it's make believe, you don't have to be afraid,
I'm right here, and make believe
can't hurt you. He knows better already
and I have to keep remembering to know
better. The dragon comes, I narrate triple-time,
slow down and draw out the victory
of those menaced, who come through
mortal risk that in the moment can only ever be real

and in the end, no casualties. How rare.
Big smiles, relief, still he put his head
under the pillow while the danger reared up,
real. Okay, but also making believe can save you,
your friends, your cosmologies, making better
belief has to be the beginning of beginning
to save you I will tell him one day, should we
get so lucky the sun rises on that day. Oh,
all along I have forgotten to say welcome.
How meat this meta cute becomes.
Welcome to these poems which are all
this, all the time, often differently, welcome
to these poems which expect you to be
in this movie with them, welcome
to this poem that knows you're a movie,
welcome, welcome to being on my sleeve,
welcome to being my heart, look
it's got a megaphone in the least
of its ventricles, another ventricle entirely
stuffed with masks and the other two,
what am I, a doctor? I miss you already,
welcome, welcome, welcome
to the belief I make, no need to stay awake,
I don't think it was your cinnamon roll
I ate, but so sorry am I nonetheless
and when I say that I trust you know
my stick figures even as they go on
bend over backwards
to say *thank you*.

meta

This is the Part of the Poem Where You Help Me Out

This is the part where I describe
                    the edges of the lake
          but not the lake

so it will be your lake I tiptoe around
                    with my scalpels
          and my markers,

with my masking tape and my staples
                    and my ideas
          about all things

insisting their way into frame. This
                    is the part
          where mountains rise

because pop-up book, because eagle-struggling-
                    to-be-born-from-a-heart·
          song, because bittersweet-battery

movie. In this part the parts depart and what remains
                    is the echo
          of what's been played.

All the stage is a world. Staging the world
                    is our awl,
          punching breathing holes

into the suffocations. This is the part
                    where the hero barks
          his forehead

coming to too fast on the bottom bunk
                    of the bed
            fronting The Brother Cave

floor display at Prepubescent Males 'R Us.
                    This is the part
            where he limps

toward the exits, feeling
                    whatever you think
            feeling wronged by inanimate

objects feels like: The smallest lightning.
                    Seventh grade shame
            in the face.

I leave it to you
                    to determine
            how the hero came to be

here, what is indicated
                    by *he*, the color
            of the unquestionably clean

shirt he wears. This is that scene. What you see
                    tells you something
            about yourself, about

your relationship to a world that finds you
                    in it. A door in you
            now and again swings open

and from the sea behind it
                    something swims
            toward you.

The next part is the part where
                        the camera of the I
            pulls back

and up: you can see that the bunk beds
                        are shaking
            or they are trembling

or they are falling slowly apart, they are
                        popsicle sticks or pillars
            on the verge of coming down

into a music
                        it takes your bent / ear
                                    to make.

Just a Bunch of Received Ideas About Mazes

I'm nothing if not an excessive reaction
to an imaginary problem.
In other words I really am
something, I think, therefore I am,
I think, intermittently intimate
with the infinite. I drink
therefore—you know how that goes.
The second Big Bang will be
noted Renaissance dilettante Frames Janco
exploding into a new universe
yes we are tired
and a literally split second previous
my mouth will be full of buttons
before the Dancin' School School of Dance,
in my back pocket a flask full
of something to tenderize the buttons.
It is not always easy. When friends
told you they thought less of you
than you thought they thought
for example. How terribly the world
rakes the felt in the glitterbang and halflight
and doubleword of this casino.
Will we ever find our way
of course we will find our way
and lose it again and again and again
walking past a bus stop. It is morning
and we must decide which game
can lay claim to having the most
of our skin in it. Or maybe just sink,
through with deciding, through with maybe.
Sometimes, though, I enjoy thinking

of all the shoes I might fill
and the sun roars once more.
Before, I told you it rained inside
our umbrellas and that wasn't made up.
On the far side of the Eastgate Foods parking lot,
an older and older man sits on the curb
facing away from the highway.
Once upon a time, there was a phone booth
there. You pushed silver into it
and a voice came out.

Semipro Air Traffic Controller

Even when I say something like
I couldn't catch your driftwood
with Satan's butterfly net, skifflekind,

I'm worried it's a worn flight path,
exhausting bother. You're right, right,
a flight path still a flight path, yeah,

try not to be an exhausting bother
but think of all the calendar Xs
we might put to better beds, sung

to superior rest. I can see you from here,
like me, barking at a mountain, telling it
to wait for the piano, waving in sunflowers

with the faces of clocks. It never stops.
As poplars go, I'm more gum
than shun. What gods we have

we are giving away. It is not wrong
to take our dance cue from the beat
of a human heart, but it is wrong

to miss the other beats reddening
the lens, cracking the window. Quickly,
so very quickly, some shape alights,

to lay a hand upon what can't be
stopped, what can scarcely be slowed.
Wheels on the ground, dawns

per second, it goes so fast
there's a bow in our throats
and not just one. There's nothing

can grease Time's palm. We will not take
even this glass of water with us.
We choose when we can choose

          even as we are distracted
      by fetching, nearly designed filth
on the windowsill

           how empty we leave it.

The Answer is Not More Reality

There is no answering for the past, it is / already
beneath the water
and sinking
until, like anything else—a conversation
at a party, a tusk, granola—disaster's decorations
bubble and froth at our feet. Look
at all the stuff:
Tinsel. Crushed cans. Viscera
of unknown provenance.
No way I'm picking that up.
There is no already beneath the water,
the party tusk is sinking
into the conversation with anything else,
we up make have to stuff
only with tongues silverer.
After the party, you rinse the bottles.
After you rinse the bottles, you set them in rows.
After they are in rows, you name them
and to all the names
you try to tell the right story. The past
can't help it, it pushes you down
on a sidewalk split by long-vanished ice.
There is enough reality here
to catapult a rhinoceros,
to cover you from head to toe,
to soak the brief paper towel you are
but tell me something that goes
bounding beyond bounds,
there has to be something unreal
to make, to mend
these broken pieces into.
This means you.

A 74-Year-Old Man with Memory Loss and Neuropathy Who Enjoys Alcoholic Beverages

I am an old man but there is gold in my glass.
I try to pretend for 30 minutes
how it must feel
to be a cornered rebel guerilla
who knows that he has come to the last place
his eyes will touch. I cannot. I cannot
but wonder if his look
grows more tender
and this is eased by not being
a person on the tip of murder's tongue.
As such.
There is a moment where I think
I am closing my eyes
but what happens is different.
There is some angle, some sagging anchor
in my deal with the atmosphere.
I cannot tell whether I am outside and 43
or inside and too cold to tell. I know
something is rising
and I can feel on my tongue my feeling
of the grandest firework just lit
and the grandest firework finished,
faded into the night. I like alcoholic beverages.
I cannot tell if it is bright
or if my eyes are open too much of the way.
The drugged up dragged down air
wrinkles the skin at the base of my throat.
I know I am cornered
and I am holding on to a glass
and I am so much older than anyone

in my family can imagine.
It is hot. Even the dirt looks sorry.
This is not the only reason
I bring the glass to my lips: I always do.
Here becomes less
a way you can bind me, less and less
a place where I might be.

The Electric is Excellent in the City

It is hard to understand why you keep singing
about banana trees, as if that
would bring them back. The city is growing
in each breath we take
while wildly we look for what to cling to.
Perhaps all we have is a different thing to say
about what lightning is. For one of us
it is the wheel of a car razoring through
the puddle, lifting a sheet of iridescent water
over the flowerbox of remaining morning papers.
For another one of us,
it is a woman in a red dress at dusk
walking without hesitation into the fountain
at the center of the city. We will never know
if she was crying. If we ever make it
to the true center of the city, we will see
a kind of heart kept aloft by a blur
of fetching lures. From the lures,
taut wires thread into each window
in each building in the city, windows
which glow and flicker and blink,
like eyes that have seen a banana tree
exactly once.

Diary of a Busy Doctor

In the present there is no time, there is a shark's fin
disappearing. This is a word I carry down the hall:

fin. I hate to wear gloves, I do hate to feel
so above you, but I cannot not. To my future self

I say *Pick up the lemonade*, to my future
executrix I say *Apportion what remains*

according to need. To the future,
I say *Be still: I only want your solutions*

waking in me, crystallizing as symphony
from crises' shrieking cacophony. Yes.

A scrip. To fetch up some quiet. There is
no present in the blade. There is no patience

below deck. I should have seen that shape
yesterday. I did, I must have, just as that shape

must not have been yesterday the shape
I should have seen. Here is an apple, it is all

I have left. There are helicopters on the roof,
who would want to live here? There is a grin

in the linoleum that won't give back
the seconds it took to notice. Say *Ah*. Here's

better light, here's a nice vest, who's for dinner
on me. Sigh *Awe*. I wish I could give you

a mask. I wish I could give your mask
a you. Give me a second—now

I push all the buttons
on the elevator.

Staggered Zebra

Every time we look up it's 1:23 or 2:22
or 1-2-3, easy as 222 miles to Louisville
now who are we going to listen to
so we'll make it through the opiate dusk?
Let it be something that hits us
into feeling, please, we are bleeding out
despairing, please let us be jolted.
That was close, the dusk
almost got us into that last bed,
instead we leapt backward
into a thunderstorm outside Nashville,
we joined Sam Cooke in song
and turned falling glass nails into glances
from an insufficiently hungry predator.
Once it's luck, twice it's luck, three times
and you have been the predator all along.
Two by two by two the wedding party
moves down the aisle
and two by two by two they return
the world subtly altered, subtly older.
We know we're not long for this yes
yes yes so let's let's let's. 123 years
from when this here first seizes into being,
it is 1889. 222 years ago it is 1790, long
romantic period to hear some diminish it
even though then one could see
one's breath in winter as evidence:
you could fill a balloon with a soul
like a cloud sphere-ing blossom. So hard to jump
anywhere but backward, staggered
as we are, zig-zagged of brain and grace.

Back then was before, now increasingly after
Biggie Smalls, but he'll always have wanted
the same thing as anyone else: numbers
to cling to, odds to confound ends, ends
that soothe means, consistent glimmer
landing us on that hook, someone trying
to show us our matter matters
and our matters meant. Have you been
a zebra like a candy glass statue
drilled by some awful hammer? You try to rise
into your brand new lean like it's a lean
you mean to. Even now, new numbers
are turning into the words for the you
you are becoming.

Available State Compensation Remedies #1:
Museum

Don't you love it when they walk toward you,
looking up into the museum's surprises?

Don't you love it when a flipped vehicle
is a particular cleverness suspended in a gallery

that worries over you, a tape recorder
on its inverted ceiling playing a language

you don't know, accompanied by unfamiliar
instruments somehow still reassuring?

Your favorite pronoun walks toward you
in a fine jacket held onto with fine hands

level with a fine, nervously-protected sternum,
the glass doors poised to swing closed

behind them. In the movie this makes
they may be a different one every time—

each exerts an awful pull. You see the car
in their wake, it remains upside down

but seems less still, you can almost
taste smoke. This must be

what it's like to be a soft, wet puppet
waking into lightning.

You can tell as the glass doors fall
back towards the building

that smeared across them
are the reflections of clouds

but you cannot untaste the smoke.
And as your one, whose one you are,

sets out across the impossibly green lawn
to meet you, you cannot put your finger on

some elusive remainder, whose failure
to appear / almost gently

      saps all color and light from the scene.

Geriatric Anesthesiology

Proceeding with delicacy is a cultivation,
sayeth the fragile and the giant.
Often, I think all that remains of each year
is a ghostly hand, writing an epistle
into the calamity quilt of our consistency.
And we are dolls made of correspondence
with time which is always running out
which is why I hate it but Hey! Look
at that shopping cart go backwards
down the incline. The haught slung
from the sun hits and passes through
and makes shadow, makes glint—
And something rises up in you
like words surging up off a page,
like the appellative scars on a tree trunk
picking up their own knives.
Is it any wonder you find yourself
on this bus, twilight indigo
leaking all over you, and in your hand
what? Doesn't it feel like a tiny jar
of teeth? What is medicine?
Be with me here, in this now.
I am imagining what it is like
to be even older, to have
what is strung together for you to play
into recognizable shape and legible meaning
begin a slow farewell. There is something
so delicate about a charred house,
the way it tells you what it was,
over and over.

Public Health Response to a Rabid Kitten—
Four States, 2007

Come here, throw pillow.
Come here, tawny flame wobbling
on the side of the road.

White coats come out of the building
like kleenex after kleenex
pulled from the tall box

by an invisible hand
and they are making the sun hurt
even more. Come here, little electron,

can't you hear the ice hissing at you?
It is the year for this kind of bend,
the things that the tumbling coats want

is taken away from them
and given to some other fear-goosed thing
and said fear-goosed thing

does not have the right hands.
Come here, unhappy bean, I know
you think you are a stone

with an itch inside. I promise you
this is only a blanket.

Knit Your Own Sweater, Boss Lady

Bridelike goes the generous smoke
from the burning banners, irked clouds
marriageable to the imaginary at last.

This is the day you let the oceanic forest fire
turned and turning inside you
emerge, a non-sequitur so white-hot

you can feel the caboose de-couple
from the train. In the aftermaths,
there is a courtesan in a blade of grass,

a can of soup in a glance, we are all becoming
genius, all become politicians of the moment—but
when to our senses will all we come?

It will be too late. The swimming pool
will already have been empty, already
past the last elegant twist

we will have achieved terminal velocity,
choice long ago ashed at the altar
of one beauty or another, one wreck or another.

And still, in a can of soup, in a courtesan,
in a burning banner: there is. A caboose.
A train. Swiftly, each paradox

like feather after feather plucked slow
will lift from our skin's ledger
and like harrowing confetti

mar the light following us. The question
before us is: how do you go?
Do you make like an awkward explosion,

a giraffe birthed onto the floor of a discothèque?
Do you gaze to the side, pensive
with all you will never have made? No,

I don't mean at the real end. I mean
now, with this question put to you:
you won't escape the punctuation

rushing up. What name
            can't you keep in your mouth?

Lester Bangs Talks Scottie

PSH (1967–2014)

It's not enough to say "sad," alright,
you need a flood. You need a line
like a serrated knife edge
to even get started, an anti-riff, like
whatever the violin that can't keep its chin up
crawling out from under the worried trombone
says in the bathroom mirror
to "Kashmir" or "Should I Stay
or Should I Go" or something, like
you take a spiral ring notebook, right? and
you fill it. You fill it with lust and shame
and real beauty and the feverish,
trembling trust you get from puppies
or babies, anybody truly new, who knows
what they need absolutely
but they're half a planet from having
any way to actually say it
but they go and wail toward it anyway, right
they wail with their mouths and their arms,
their thighs, it's a caterwaul attacked by
another caterwaul in the dark, it's coming
from the cheese-brained hearts
at their crying, lurching, gaping, hoping
centers—you call it cock, you call it cunt,
you call it yearning, kissing
as a respiratory emergency, it's like
waking up on a beach, what beach?
I don't know / *nobody* fucking knows,
you get more clinical if you have to
but *that's* the notebook
and then you rip the metal spiral out

and you put the paper in the driver's seat
of a stupid car / you almost want
the car to kiss the boy and everyone
watching they didn't even know
they could want the boy to be kind
to this other boy, this off-kilter, discomfiting
boy, yawn and sigh made flesh
like an Orange Julius with feelings
until they see what's left, and you know
technically the metal spiral can be
threaded back through and restore
the notebook to being a notebook,
technically, that flaming, wrinkled,
ink-stabbed hope chest
but it's not the same notebook
and you know it / the pages don't turn
the bottoms of significant moments curl
and disintegrate in a dirty mist
and it's as bad as you think,
it's worse and then there's seeing it and being
another human, fucked and wired to love
and protect whatever we think we are
to the point of inventing murdering
who we aren't, who we are / we are so
embarrassed, dumb want is the long shadow
of every light in the cosmos
stuffed into short shorts a size too small
and how is that pain beautiful
to us, how is that beauty so disgusting?
Oh Scottie. Is that the upset apple cart
of questions you leave us with,
like a pile of 8-tracks with goo all over it,
is it some other order of intervention?
How much Scottie can you stand, I mean
how much Scottie can you stand
to recognize you are?

Bereavement Company Picnic

And then shall the wolved much serenade,
and then shall the other thing much happen too,

no? As a specialist in grief recovery,
I am qualified to make of such qualms

claims. *Do not think all ecstasies the same!*
says the thundercloud pelting the alleys

with ridiculous dictionaries, *Nor boiling water
all the same!* though at times

it has/will have been: oft
does its sameness seem mighty.

You may ask what a Bereavement Company is.
You may ask, cocking your head, *Why for?*

But such a company may ask of you:
no one knew we needed a mechanical

washer of dishes nor a robot
to fetch our prescriptions,

right? and now look. I recover
grief, the hole out of which oceans

and wars &c. I serve the humans, now one
who sucks blood from the new divot in his thumb

where he got into a physical reality disagreement
with the cheese grater and, turning, finds no one

beside him in the kitchen. The cheese
seems tougher tonight, but it is your heart.

I list with a pewter tankard through such blues
but that's the job. There's a metal taste,

a stillness in the foyer rudely golded
by relentless days into which less and less

and more and more of us will wake.
Those cries in your heels, the plucked keys

of your despair which is always becoming
another version of itself

or bugling into an altogether
altogether else. I list with a tankard growing lighter

until I can see the big tent lose
its crutches, the slow plunge that looks like

it wouldn't hurt a noncombatant hemophiliac:
it is so different beneath

than seen from afar. Saying tent is just my way
of talking about it, my safe image.

We think these sounds will act like wolves
I mean shields I mean

oxygen masks with scabbards holding sharp swords
to cut the failing tent away

      but it is really just beginning.

Bereavement Company Christmas Party

We plunge through wreaths of sparks here
and into the event, all maw, all belly, all eyes,
all appetite and process but shortly

the photographs, taken out of
some pathological need
will be as veils to what we see:

two empty champagne bottles, tiny lungs
teetering on a table, upside down broken jaw,
two coworkers kiss with furious, cutting tears

beneath a copper sprig wet with blood.
This part of the song is sawed in half
by the shark, the punch in the bowl

strained through rags retired
from swabbing wounds. The toy Doberman
does not care for us, the dowdy executrix

wags her gilded pipe at our loosened ties
like scarecrow legs trembling from tree limbs,
the ordnance arrives shortly after

the tiny bathtubs brimming with whiskey
and voices through the ventilator shafts twine
minor chords so that we are sure

someone is being mourned, someone is always
being mourned. Then of course we realize Jesus,
then we realize God, no, gods

with many heads, no, devils blown out
of the faces of mountains, our representatives,
then the necklaces made from teeth

of those we survive and rhapsodize over,
humming in elevators. We are dizzy
with the gone, the broken branches,

our outsides worn smooth. The first drops of rain
seem startling then having to walk
the long parking lot, the cloudburst is so there

it nearly isn't. All the boxes beneath the tree are open
and before we go to our efficient conveyors
we will detour first to a place for stowing

such gifts deep below the ground,
where our eyes will no longer be touched.
Moving on, we practice believing

we will no longer be touched. This is
a real party, even stopping it doesn't stop.
Every ventilator shaft breathes

sadder. We will wake if we wake
singing or sobbing into the threshold
where our business becomes the world.

Bereavement Company (0): At the Grief Recovery Academy

Here we indulge our full grief
and take notes, we gauge the flex of sorrow,

the way it lives in muscle, the way it licks
briar-tongued upside your softness, how

it makes of the lung a sandbag
barbed by an impossible lure. We tabulate,

we make charts, there is lunch.
We skate in the afternoon

in the period of suspended weeping,
creasing awhile in the suggestive air.

Once you step through the turnstile
and achieve the metal detector,

you must answer to all you can carry
from the darkest rooms.

They ask you and ask you
like you swallowed a shovel

they are taking back, until nothing
belongs to you, until you ask yourself

in the practiced manner of an assassin
or nurse and even then

it's only possible to tell
that where now there's a stale taste

there was once a grief
preening like an awkward lily

that may any second blossom
into the head of a dragon.

meta

Gizmo Idolatry

Is malady the greater genius at survival
or is it the coping apparatuses
we outfit our hope with
right in malady's face?
We think machines will save us
right up until we know better
but the worlds we may save
exist in those animals
we have christened seconds
and in the parts of those seconds
we name as though in a fever—.
Still, there's nothing so flying
it can't be made to crash.
Take a very specific example:
a used, metal, off-white Swingline stapler
flies through the air. It is really flying,
look at it go. But then there is
a toy helicopter and a boy dressed
in a lion suit holding the toy helicopter
and the boy is interested in flying
mostly as preamble to catastrophe.
This is the part
where the boy lion knows
something will go wrong.
There are those ready to call his urge
a malady that crooks and stunts.
the deep seed of compassion
that may blossom in us for instance
when we take someone's hand
as our helicopter dips and flails
awkwardly into something that looks like

and cannot be a giant stapler
flying through the sky. How
can this have happened?
We are riding in a helicopter.
Just a moment ago
we pointed out a gleam in the ocean
beside the rocks, a flash of light
we were certain was a seal.

Concept

Here is the big thing and here is the little thing
the big thing encounters. The clock radio
crows some mid-period Prince.
The curtain blows into the room
like the cape of a departing hero
even though the window is painted shut. Good
morning. The little thing encounters
the big thing. What "extra time"? What
"kiss"? It is possible to make out
the sound of the filament in the light
overhead, sighing at a sprint
which is a soft way to understand
burning. There may be a loaf of bread
just baked, some urgency seems to move
from room to room, some urgency at work
in the big thing
although also completely divorced
from it and still also
clicking and buzzing in the little thing.
What calls out to us when we are the big thing
to take the little thing and discover
how quickly we may separate the little thing
from even its most benign curiosities?
The big thing spins and the little thing
tries to push back the sheets. The big thing
tries to push back the sheets and the little thing
nods antennae like drumsticks during
an ostentatiously quiet solo. The big thing
nods its antennae and the little thing
does something so little the notion of time
lifts like a skiff of fluff on the wind,

the kiss of a weathered postcard glimpsed
briefly—Some afternoons seem to burn
right through the roof, the filaments in the sky
pressing hard overhead. The house where I grew up
survives fitfully in these reaching fragments,
where I ran my hands over such beautiful little things
even as something big I still don't understand
kept happening.

Voice-Over

She walked across the room like a swan
on an oil-slicked river licking through
a scorched city, she crossed the room walking

bi-pedal, like a human, toward the desk /
the wardrobe / the abyss like she'd heard a lot
said of her, over her, a thousand times

too many. She talked like smoke
purring into a ravine where you
had just gone missing. You try being a *femme*

fatale in a world full of chewing gum
commercials. Shadows chiaroscuro, so many
rules, you try being a *femme vitale*

in a world where she walks and talks her story
into a story I would be the last to tell.
There was some interference. She walked like,

talked like and like. She asked for help like she was
in a movie. The movie should have asked
for help. It was clear I was some

interference. Clear as that kite
in your memory of almost swooning
to death off a cliff overlooking the Pacific,

the Pacific like a beckon of glass muscle
which is to say fronting clarity while all the while
something never not murk. Not my scene

but I walked on anyway: I stopped caring
whose marks I hit. It was like being in the movie
playing on the television in the background

of the antepenultimate scene of a movie
you think I remember explaining to you. She said
I had a gift for analogies but analogies

were a poor substitute for a disjunctive
syllogism. Something something murder, blah blah
blackmail, something else stocking agleam

as wet, white paint on the palest clematis
ruckused by a ribboned lattice of cigarette smoke
breezing through. You could see it plain

as the soon-to-be-broken nose on any passing face:
she walked not yet talking west
across the model of destiny manifest

that was the bargain carpeting, talking by walking
she walked into talking before she even opened
her mouth. She talked like debris

in a champagne flute before she smoothed
her hand from her glove then smoothed her glove
from her hand. Any beginning explodes,

every introduction springs violently
in all directions like a horse with a thorn
in its lion, like an echo talking back,

a preliminary understanding of how the world
feeds on us, walking, she says *Hello*, *Hello* she says
like someone stepping out of an airplane cargo bay

in a dinner dress like cold black coffee poured over
the *ballerina segunda*. This scene is really all
that talking, we might as walking

be talk between two different fingers
on the ceiling of the Sistine Chapel. I'll allow my talk
was walk, my ear bent, tongue detective

and crooked, I mean she really said *Hello*, things
were livened up considerable, as I saw them, her
hell. She balked at the office of my office,

I made all the talk of her *Hello* a plank
walk, stalk of echo, the long goodbye
of any startle, any start, any star—

Bomb Shelter

You shouldn't hurt anyone or anything, that's easy
& then there is the rest of your life.
You avoid the hot thing, yes,
but everything seems to emanate from the hot thing.
Then to hurt early so as to not hurt as much
later. Then to be inside the hot thing
until you are the hot thing
making the hot thing happening
a whisper of perpetuity, a suggestion.
You shouldn't hurt anyone if you can help it,
the hot thing says. You shouldn't hot any hurt one,
says thing help, yes. Yes, quite nice to talk
plastic cup tea party / the pox of the politics of language
but then you learn the rules of order
& damn hot thing hurt anyone until
sick of it are the hot hurt things wearing
self outfits enough! although never
enough, never—here's what:
you bring the fork to the mouth & it's
hot thing or not hot thing.
You make the impossible sentence
& not the meal really but still perhaps the hot thing
or not the hot thing. I feel like eating my foot
right off my body. What doesn't make me feel this
is the hot thing. As when some shadow
like a hand streaks through the proceedings
& everyone does a quarter-turn.
As when there's an everyone to go doe-eyed
& to go doe-eyed over.
All of a sudden we can see the buildings again,
or the farmhouses, or the kinked tinsel

like a snake tongue wagging from the dirt.
Silly in the wind. Someone has clearly been
here, someone is. We are not dead yet.
Look at that thing they did. Look how hot
it sounds, look at us looking as though
through a cloud bleeding imperatives,
a mist hissing *quick quick quick*!
Come quick! and we're quick
and not yet dead.

This Song's About a Superhero Named Tony: It's Called "Tony's Theme"

Something's beginning to emerge
from the belfry of our wishing, I know it is,
something that will take a shape
that before had only been suggested
peripherally, something that will shed
its somethingness as it crystallizes
from what it could to be
into what it definitely is. Today,
we want little: maybe a cold beer
to amp early Spring's crisp light,
but then the giant bells start tolling—
tolling that makes the trees look nervous,
tolling that shakes the ground underneath us
and it's like being in love while bound
and gagged and upside down, the *cri de cœur*
struggling to escape the swaddle of the body
then circling back in like a torched buzzard.
Each bell nod slings a fierce interrobang,
griefs pulling the hair of shadows.
Now we are on our knees,
asking for something. This something
I will call Tony. As in Where is Tony
when you need him? As in Tony
can you hear me? Fire engines
pass ambulances, the risen traces
of our histories bear down on us,
the tulips betrayed by winter's second wind,
wake avalanching forward, overtaking
fake spring. Tony, Tony, Tony,
if you weren't there
you would never believe me.

After the Film Adaptation of Bobby Gaugin's
Tricycle! Waterfall!, w/ Off-Brand Orange Juice

Bear with me—I am about to create an epiphany
and there will probably be some spilling
perhaps a small fire
no I am kidding: this is about the time
I went to see a movie
and by "went" I mean I crossed from the kitchen
into the fur bowl of the living room
and hacked away the blinds in a fit of peek. Suddenly,
a remote control in my hands, the eyes of a pack animal
looking back at me. Or I was at a museum
or I was at the mechanic's and seeing this thing
the surface of which had been with unsettling intensity
mussed. I looked at this thing
as if watching a movie in a library built
from the dreams strangers can't help
but tell you. *Bang!* Epiphany. This spring
spoke directly to me
and it said something you may never share
the understanding of *Bang!* It was shaped like its shape
then like a cannonade of its shapes
flying over a crowd of cowed socialites
or a crimson ribbon leashed to the launched skull
of an erstwhile bear beside a green unfinished.
Perhaps mundanely it was revealed that none in the world
can ride a tricycle out of a waterfall, but
this is only true if the waterfall, tricycle, and rider
conform to limited expectations. The tricycle seems like a symbol
but then it starts talking. I realized
that how it whispered to me
belonged only to me

but I tried to give it to you anyway,
even though the best I could do was repeat the whisper
in words I came up with, a mantra, a reversed
curse, a little tenderness
tried. The cashier was being unbelievably patient:
I had forgotten how I count. *Bang!* And as the spaceship
went into the mountain, as the man with the walkie-talkie
and the gold-buttoned blazer approached me,
as I stood in my living room feeling as if I were falling
already, I said something perfect enough
that it no longer felt like describing a motion
of my cartoon mind obscuring the empty sky,
it felt like it sounded like *Bleep, bleep, Void,*
I am coming for you
next.

Fan Mail

Those hair extensions look so real, everything
looks so real about you like so real
the logical explanation can only be

you got a time machine and went backwards,
to the sepia days when your hair was longer
and cut your hair from the past

to make extensions with and now it's so
real-looking it's like not having hair extensions
at all, oh my god. And effects so real are like

real, like almost totally real, right, so my question is
in two parts: a) where do I get a time machine
and b) do you really set fire to your co-stars

or representative portraits of your co-stars
without warning? Like, they come to set one day,
maybe an early morning call, maybe a midnight

shoot and then it's like INT: *fade in on [you,*
or something that looks a lot like you] totally on fire
all of a sudden. We need to know these things, it's vital

we know what we'd otherwise just suspect
like it's important to be able to kill everybody
and their families and cripple any potential future

families a million times over, right,
like that's what makes a *country*—but I digress.
Remember the hippopotamus who was your friend

and made all those unpleasant yet humorous
quips? Write me back, write me
in your own blood. c) don't I own you, and c)

do I not own you? c) will you lie down
with me? What do we have to know? What
do we have? This nuclear winter

will be *our* nuclear winter. You can trust me,
I'm always the one saying you're not a snake
unless you are playing a snake which is when

I let everyone know how great a snake you are/were
like the realest, greatest snake, oh my god.
O, can't someone just press the button

already? I knew a woman who stripped
the cotton from my eyes, the light
like a deep breath drawn in the Arctic.

I knew a woman, I had a life, it's true
then it changed once I realized you were
embellishing it. Like I was imagining you taking

an arctic breath and I couldn't see myself
taking an arctic breath and now what's real
is less. The gauze crimsoned, the horizon

nearing, is it like this for you? I was the only one
who got how genius it was for you
to add ventriloquism to the rogue police detective

who is secretly the moral center of the pre-apocalyptic
world that writhes and feeds as though the apocalypse
has come and gone without saying goodbye

and I'm like "Is this even a movie?"
The thrown voice underlines the lack
of individual agency and plus it was weird

but in a cool way. I like lettuce do you like lettuce
why don't you like lettuce like I like lettuce?
I'll sleep at the foot of your bed

but I can't promise I'll sleep.
Do you really know what it's like to be
a private detective/ice cream magnate/father,

or are you pretending? I thought we could go
on a ride. You could pretend it into a balloon ride.
I can pretend us into the celestial metropolis

you thought was just a trick of the light
once light was combined with the *gratis* cocktail
waiting in your trailer. I thought maybe

I could be the *gratis* cocktail waiting
in your trailer, I thought maybe I could
lope through your green screens, my eyes

like tongues like fingers watching you,
like the lord and like the lord I will always want
in, to step out of the backdrop, to step out

from the dust and the light fiddling the dust
into little suggestions—d) I need a wink a lightning
rod a prayer stage-whispered, ticking beneath

the catchphrase, beneath the tweaked defiance
a split second before you open a portal
or find the missing dog or turn over the impossible

poker hand, which means everything will be
after all alright. I never turn over
the impossible poker hand. I alone prowled

the message boards with a deep sense of how real
it was for you to be garbed in Victorian regalia
on the trail of a monocled demon

who fed exclusively on the hearts of desiccated animals
and blonde college freshmen. Now I need you
to do the same for me.

Fan Mail 2: Nanny Time Approacheth

After the nuclear war, the only people left
will be ex-celebrities and out-of-work nannies

I expect, and my intuitive calculations
concerning nannies are never wrong, totally—

mildly errant would be a better way to describe
my intuitive calculations concerning nannies,

a gift I discovered after your turn as a nanny
who brokers a cessation of hostilities

in the Middle East—a farce with no superheroes
in it, in this day and age, oh my god—via

much toughness and falling down
and exaggerated accents and a fat, gold,

democratic heart. Or brain. It must be said,
I am less accurate when it comes to

ex-celebrities. Sometimes at work I find
I am drawing a picture of your heart

only it looks like a fat brain, it's gold
but it's damned democratic and then

I am inventing new colors for it, gold
is not enough, oh my god. The *Times* found you

cloying, I find the *Times* a cinderblock
covered in moldering oatmeal and anyway

those of us who understand
the secret hardiness of true nannies

know better. Now: who writes your red carpet?
What will you say after the nuclear war?

When it happens I think everyone
should pretend it never happened—red carpet

will chase the horizon, and we will need
to say many meaningless things.

Sometimes you seem sweaty
and completely dry at the same time

and I feel that this will come in handy
as we begin to rebuild. You might say

that nuclear winter is where nannies
separate the wheat from the chaff, the nannies

from the babysitters. Life will grow
more competitive: fewer children, greater

tasks, the gathering of groceries
suddenly Herculean and violin lessons

an exercise in nerve-harsh
that would dismantle utterly

the most frozen-veined black operative.
You know, like the one you played

in your first comeback, the one
whose dismantlement by a random children's

violin recital first made me feel
like all the missiles could launch

and still something would be, in the end
or after, okay. Or that we could act like it was

so convincingly, it almost
would be.

Tracking Shot

Whose anti-aircraft battle station this is
I think I know, the deliquescing snow falling
like tears falling from a floating motorcade. Night

builds its walls: outside its badminton nets, inside
its jury boxes full of foxglove and ash. *It is all right,*
says the sunlight stapled to the floor

but was I not just passing an anti-aircraft battle station
and then suddenly in an empty courtroom
with lickably-named flowers sitting at night

in the place where citizens once fanned themselves?
More and more, I'm certain I have ruined
Christmas. More and more, every anywhere

through which I move seems poignantly condensing
as if I'd been called upon to swim through lead triangles.
Whose auburn-lit afterparty this is

I think I have reason to fear. Where for instance
are the chips? Am I right to be suspicious?
The world does not expand in the way we think

but in the where we think. The miles it makes
it cannot make except that they are inside us.
More and more whose light-pen I seek

I wish I knew, whose architectural digest were fit
to fit the outsides crowding me
into the marble sack of beautiful dioramas inside of me

I long for, as I long for you, your touch
like a swirl of choreographed pine needles
dimpling a hot water bottle,

a charm against feeling

     I will never be home.

Gust Avrakotos Pulls Lancaster Dodd's File in the CIA Archive, 1989

PSH (1967–2014)

Sooner or later you realize: every tragedy of the last century
is at least partly a story of the failure
of power to account for its own sustenance.
Look, don't be dumb: existential threats never really end,
they just get managed. For every epic,
winter, babies, etc. Vacuums grow pricks like mushrooms / E.g. "the
    Master":

> *You seem so familiar to me.*
> *We are not helpless, and we are on a journey*
> *that risks the dark. Who likes you, except for me?*

You forget how you got to any peak? then suddenly the Zen master's
"We'll see" has more murderous edges, a century
of knives broken into smaller, sharper knives. The epic
really is in the fiefdoms of all these little pricks, the constant
    failures
to realize how to maintain an infrastructure that doesn't beg for an
    end—
Power? Power can't *wait* to be an idiot, you know? "I. AM.
    SUSTENANCE":

> *Go to that landless latitude, and see.*
> *If you figure out a way to live without a master, any*
> *master, let us know.—So familiar to me . . .*

Oh what a fucking *hack*—and not for nothing, but *sustenance*
is compromise. That shouldn't be hard. You don't need a master's
degree in geopolitical divination to see that the end

of the illusion of freedom is the end of the hope of freedom. Each
    and every century
has an endless scroll of people's harrowing failures
to not destroy other people, epic after epic after sorry fucking epic.

> *Above all, I am a man . . . hopelessly*
> *inquisitive man, just like you. If you leave—*
> *Who likes you except for me?*

I don't use the word "titanic" casually, but that's the epic
scale of a narcissism we're talking about here: to *play* commander,
    less sustenance
than seed of drought to the people whose failures
you have to weaponize just trying to master
the crushing fears you convince yourself have—*for centuries*
of millennia—plagued your specialness. How you loathe that you will
    end.

> *I don't ever want to see*
> *you again. You are asleep.*
> *You see so familiar to me.*

There's no reason this can't be fun, Lancaster. The end?
You gotta see it as a punchline / so epic
it takes the better part of a disastrous century
to land. What's *key* is having people left who can laugh; *that*
    sustenance
cannot be overvalued. You gotta undermine masters, would-be
    masters,
you have to make of their precious industry / ostentatious fucking
    failures.

> *Your spirit was free—*
> *I give you facts a trillion years*
> *in the making. Who likes you except for me?*

When failures
end
the masters
we have room for new epics,
period. Just let *sustenance*
be the first word of our rebuilding, just / give us more centuries—

> *A grilling, this. Your worries. Leave—free*
> *winds—your memories—a four and a half month siege—*
> *. . . Familiar seem-so, you see to me.*
> *Ex-me. Except for. Who likes you / accept me.*

You got me there, Lanc: I'm fucking tired. No centurion for the
    bosses, me. Failure
is always a plurality. Rage smart and hard for sustenance, it all still
    ends.
We'll see: the epic is there is no epic. The only future has no
    masters.

Some Little Movie

Lousy with suicides
the unicycle paths, lousy

with sprung umbrellas
the Olympic pool

and I am dismantled
by the love I suspect

in the air, I hear the ocean
in your question,

yeah, yeah and beside
the crosswalk, a man

playing the accordion.
This can be one movie.

This can tattoo
one thousand little movies

like a window shattered
into a delta of glass

teeth. Sequins. Freckles.
The man is young,

the man is wearing
a facsimile of the hats

worn by those bent
on ascending the Alps

in movies about
ascending the Alps.

I fix something
and two other somethings

break. You know this,
you know what it is

to walk all the way home
carrying a live coal,

tripping through
an upset reliquary

like a clumsy risk
whose equilibrium

has never not
been crippled.

You know I won't stop
asking by breathing

to carry this cup
as far as you want.

make-belief

Kite Shepherd (0)

                              ranges shovel-winged

through narrow alleys like fields,

sprints beside such dazzle and flying

and disasters among the trees
standing like burnt forks:

There are so many gods to pay off

we will never rightly beg enough
                              of them all.

In the meantime,
the meantime
                    and what we gather,
                    what we set flying,
                    what we bring more or less
                                        safely
back to earth.

Kite Shepherd (1)

I was a spark ferried by a catastrophe of wind
then I was a little girl who loved the Beatles more

than dessert's inverted chandeliers.
I pawed at the monster

slicking up the spooked conduit of my neck
then stirred frantic, unwrecked, a little boy

in a little red incorrigible wagon. A tiger
in a land of no tigers. The word was *careen*,

the word was *career*. Now

I am in love with my friends, they are distilleries
funneling puddles into celestial bodies, O

and O: I am protective and aghast, pianos
and necklaces so near the rotor blades,

so lovely and interfering
with the dangerous methods
                              of ascent.

Kite Shepherd (2)

You lounge dapper in the ante-room.

The ante-room is full of things
that seem, like afterthoughts, to mean you

no harm. Seemed. There,

before you entered the conditions
of the larger room, the narrowing elaborations

of the house, one could be or care for

anything, even when anything was catastrophically
aloft, more than enough

to make one feel one's interior life as a city

that had already been burned
to the ground, and so one's body then

a vehicle pushed into soaring

      by rushing shoulders of dark smoke.

What Isn't Rubble

There's so much poison we have to
dance. The bunny appears in bald daylight,
it's a warning! but we can't stop
pawing and why would we? Music
curls out of the air like the skin of a tree
becoming a canoe. What isn't rubble
was. In the zoo the bars are for everyone
and the rockets are in our eyes pulling us away
from even the ice cream drinks
we're using as the briefest of sweet anchors.
Remember when the porch swing creaked
a counterpoint to whatever we sang
and whatever we said in between
the singing? Even if we know better now
we still stand in a desolate parking lot
with a hand full of plastic flowers
or an accordion or a promise whispered
into a fist when sometimes what we need
is to go ahead and sink to our knees,
ruining this pair of pants forever.
What isn't rubble can be a garish sign
alerting you to the convenience of this store.
Just now you remember where you are
but not as well where you have come from.
The end is in anything that has
a chance of breaking your heart.
Sometimes it is Tuesday or you think it is
and difficult to stand as you are convinced
that swollen others rain broken stone wheels
on your kin and made family from a great height.
The sky sounds of awful laughter

but what is not rubble persists. The nipple
sings back to you on your tongue.
Her hair's a handhold lofting you above
such indifferent voids. You, also,
may be a ladder. On the wood bench outside
the bookstore the birds insist
like a frantic choir as you open
your friend's new book. All these cries
might be rubble. You might be
forgiven for backing away, and turning.
That's none of my business. Telling you
about being split open and building
a fortress of light into that split—Hell,
I have no business. Here, let me spit
that safety pin into your hand.
It's the key to a city to which
we must be on our way.

Marching Band Adjudication Services

You do not see us, but we move among you
with our special lenses and very small
notebooks. Once in a great while,

a part of us will grow fond
and rush to cradle the elbow
that is about to give beneath your sousaphone

just to see you gleam and sound
against the dark of the sky's decaying teal.
Yes: even those charged with the rigorous

application of standards grow weak
trying to bear the terrible negotiations of energy
with shapes such energy rushes against.

Some call us angels. We are
only given to say how far
into the air got the sound

you asked to move through
such puzzles of brass and wood and flesh
and skin pulled tight—

                    In a previous life

I remember moving through an expensive restaurant
with more of my kind. Candles in rows desperately licked
at thorny crystals hung from above:

the light rivered along the white, white tablecloths
of the empty tables as we swept
toward the porch in the back

to eat beyond our means, always beyond
our means, beneath the questions crickets
chisel out of quiet

                          when the lights go out.

Veteran Kid

He drives around a lake 13 times. He drives
around the same lake another 14 times
for a glance he hopes detonates

into one specific future and it doesn't so he drives off
forever and never throws another thing away.
Of her tricycle, she never lets go,

even as she looks away from the road,
tall, making believe the cars behind her
make the sound of waves. We make

mountains of what makes us, almost never
not the child. She never let go, she never
rode. Scraps fly through the air

of who everyone else was and is,
a thousand thousand endings wending
the forked way lightning has, never alone

and never not. So we are bruised and split,
oozing from rift, reft of lift, iffy produce? And?
He didn't know he was still alive

until he wasn't. He was the primary eroding agent
cutting listing paths through hillsides of receipts
and postfunctional tabulation devices.

Then he wasn't, and others were sent in
to clean up. When we say kid we always think
we know what we mean. A dozen trumpets

fall to the floor. He looked at the piano
he might have played. The fresh-cut grasses
of Missouri in early December said

almost no one. Here, *almost no one*
is another center for every other one.
Thing after thing snaps. She has

difficulty knowing with precision what it is
for which she grieves. There is a paper heart
in her hand that feels like a fib given

shape, its leash broken, its desires a fib
broken as any fever. Have you ever hit a bird
with your car on the first bone-cold day

of winter? He has. How awful
to take something out of the air
so far from its zenith.

Calming Measures Ahead

You start from something true enough
and then build out one entire world.
Morning is whenever you decide morning
is. You are 20 you are 80 you are
6 and just like that there are 3 worlds
asking to be given a legitimate body
teeming with teams of teeming teens
and shrubbery. And seas. And superheroes.
But ahead are calming measures,
the leash of gravity, the leash of time,
the kiss of mortal cognition.
We write into the surf. The styli we are
ride into each surface what would perish
otherwise without a sound.
Such wheels in your hands, such hands
in your eyes, such disappearing
ice. A sound bridge is not always a sound
bridge. I know it's burning when I can smell
burning. The sky is blurple it's always blurple.
Unless it's yellorangine, always it's night.
Pieces of paper seem to menace you.
Fuck "seem to": they absolutely terror-grill
you. Just like that you have a dream no
a trilogy of dreams in which you are
accompanying the husband of your friend
across many lands to try to bring her
safe home. Words weigh almost nothing,
but they beckon worlds like dense stones
shook from a universe begun as a monolith
with zero pores. Is our urgency prayer
or does our urgency prey? Hello, maker.

Make this vase pretty, prettier,
prettier still while it tells you
what you believe, what a life looks like.
I was born to never leave the spot
where I remain close to you.
You were born to move on
after watching all my tongues die down,
you say, but how can you mean it?
How severally you can mean anything:
meaning anything severs.
I pour warm sand into the wine glass
and wait. It has been that kind of day.

Good Party

Everyone survived, and some of us
danced. You came up with a cure.
It seemed so obvious, in retrospect.
It was an indescribable relief.
The lights were blue and tiny
and not slapping us in the face
as our conversations continued
despite the odds
like breezes over twitching musculatures.
At one point there was an entire zoo
inside our one friend's longing,
watching was like seeing scores of pairs
wobble off the boat onto dry land
like an upset bucket of pears. Aluminum
bucket. Hard, green pears.
Everyone survived, we counted.
We double-checked. When suddenly
the music stopped, a well-turned phrase
lifted a sentence right in front of us:
it so sparkled that even the snacks
were refreshed, what once were letters
shook their wings, a moment of fueling
before we fell into each others' arms.
The party started to look like life
in the movies, the old movies
whose arcs glittered before being
hobbled and dashed by shushing curtains.
What was that cure? Oh
how I miss you, you who know
who you are or maybe not. Once more
we fall into each others' arms, felled

and still falling, even the next morning
felled and still falling,
falling still.

At the comestible wedding

we are all terrified. What at first
seems a waiting deliciousness
is the family of the bride. What seems
a field of jerky are the boys grimacing
and hung over beside the groom.
So much presentation
the competing presentations
must weather each other while waiting
for meats & cheeses various
to slalom down the aisle, and look!
they've fretted the arch with actual
neuroses! It is autumn, there is candy
the color of a waning campfire
in the trees. Will they make it?
is a question that sometimes prods one
from sleep even while dreaming
of flying from a pleather vacation
aboard an elite cruise liner
to a journalism job interview. Who says
the past doesn't exist? is
another question one asks
when wondering why make it
they did not, but there are
other examples, there have to be
other stories, where the burger
is perfect and the golden rings
are a sustaining resource. Here
we are, eaten and being eaten even now,
cooling and coalescing into flavors
more subtle and subtler still.
Will we make it? We are married food

after all, waiting to be devoured.
Are we really at the comestible wedding?
I thought there would be more hats.
Still, the sun stays buttered on the proceedings
and the way the bride and groom look
at each other, dish to dish!—like how fast
we disappear doesn't matter,
all that matters is extending this now,
this meal which all light falls into.

There are 21 dogs on the *To Be Destroyed* list

and the journey of a single step disappoints
a thousand miles in all other directions. My dream
of rescue helicopters and sleighs is related to you, dogs

at risk of destruction, but as much to you,
alert citizen. Just think, if I started right now
I could probably make it

to where you are whoever you are
though you might be already gone
in some unforgivable way, where you were

remembering you only as seven dozen balloons,
each cluster the beginning of a city
in a new world I could walk towards forever

and never get to. Can we soften *nasty, brutish
and short*? Maybe, maybe not, still I feel
like I'm coughing up teeth

and I will never get where we could be going.
There are 21 dogs on a list with a name
that has been rendered by flushing ink

into precise wounds and this softens
not me, but also it is true that we are all
on that list. We were beauties, too,

weren't we? We thought we were waiting
in cages that moved like train cars
slowing through a town less a town

than the refugee camps we'd been taught to despise.
Maybe we waited in no such cages, maybe
we never didn't. The journey of one

is a journey of a thousand maybes
cut into by the shrapnel of the voice, the debris
of loving, the heat lightning of a look

crossing a room. I would only have it
many other ways. I want to take a tent
out of my chest full of dancers and acrobats

and a determined, swift girl
who moves from pre-coffin to pre-coffin
to free and lead those to-be-destroyed dogs

like balloons in a stiff wind
to the beach: some will float out over the sea,
others will comb back just ahead of the ebb

until they amble into the city, briefly
well again. The rest remain, trembling
with unmade song, on the shifting lip

where solid ground becomes beauty unthreading
like a slow catastrophe, like clockwork,
like they were born to it.

The Devil is in the Details, God is in the Details, the Devil is God

It has been so long since I shimmied up
to your carnival booth, O lord,
although it has not been so long
since the cuss of shadow
came back upon mine
like a snapped chain.
You are of use when you are a goat,
trembling down the road out of town
with the realized sorrows of the town
bound to you. Something has to pay
or rather something has to play-act the pay-out
those quiet and indiscernible teeth
cut from us. Tonight my friend
is waiting a horrible wait, tonight his hands
are folded over what cannot be helped.
When the boat pulls away
from the motionless man
into the dark, moonless waters,
I am trying to watch him, am trying
to listen for some note or seven to join
in answer. Instead my glance angles up:
it is you, like a feather folding over pocket watch.
Like smoke where there's no fire
nodding, nodding
and backing away.

This Will All End In Tarantulas, I Know It

and it can be hard to know anything else
though we try harder than that all the time
to make beliefs we insist secure us.

You could be standing in a thick, dark night
raked by hovering helicopters.
Their nervous searchlights trace the city blocks

in disappearing squares you think
for a second you are the center of.
You could blink it all away, blink it

all back. "It" could be a phone
conversation that feels like a bear
pawing your prone form

while your insides go berserk
remembering inhaling margarita sno-cones
against the giant shoulder

of Texas summer. Such shadows, they
are forever in my mouth until I think
how shadows could be filled with spiders

until I further think how soft they would be
if they just remained motionless and now
I can't stop shouting. How far does your arm

reach? Isn't there something a little further
that you want? You could be kneeling beside
the open mouth of a bomb bay, the falling teeth

nearly silent, dumb tumbling, baby acrobats.
I hope you aren't. What bright tarantulas
result, after all. What gaudy parasols they throw

over each of their shoulders, tethered to you now
with a leash you'll never let go.

Abridg'd Epic

First the thing but before that thing
another, much-maligned thing
which caused the *in medias res* thing
to come into being which, in the irony
that powers the cartwheeled *mise-en-scène*
that is the angularly ballooning universe,
it would be the fate of said middle thing
to reverse then reverse again—Still with us?
There was blood, lots of it. The monsters
got smaller, but the damage
got bigger, ships were built for so long
some of them went into the sky.
Oceans were crossed, some had stars in them,
we all had stars in us, mirrors were
fought, somewhere in there
kindergarten. Next, the thing—traumatic
or no, it was quite a thing and it altered the river
if you get my meaning. The architecture
of nests advanced as the debris proliferated
as if all the thing-doers were geniuses
primarily of the undoing of things.
If the hazmat suit fits, &c.
There was a boy, there was a girl, there was
an entity who wished not to be identified
save as visible solely at an angle
through the cracks and fissure that appeared
in the tapestries depicting things big and little
connected connected connected like the yarn
that makes up all balls of yarn.
No leering, thank you.
You humans with your names and tags.

There was a name on the spectrum
whose yearning got weaponized,
there was an entity, there was
a longed-for lusted after
at an unacceptable distance
isn't there always? Entity the Sky Thing,
entity the Tribe, entity the State, the Self,
the Plot, not necessarily in that order
but not not. Stuff was delicious
before the air got hammered into shape
rattling through the mouth cut into
the sound *delicious*. And here we are, declaring
stuff delicious: fate! I would be remiss
to leave out the helicopters, that Helen,
that other Helen, that Helen that was
the systemic oppression of a variety
of exploited underclasses, that monster
and that monster's mother, that search
for parentage, we went through a land
and it was so hot, it was so cold,
it wasn't even a land we went through.
We went generally in search of specifics
and there they were, everywhere, a downy wing
floating to the floor of the hot attic,
a jump rope coiled beside a drain in the showers
of the penitentiary, a bowling ball in a flowerbed,
some awesome ghastly music not unexpected
except in the form in which it arrived
i.e. totally unexpected. Before a hot mic,
yes, an accident not at all an accident
and so many custodial dead because of.
The dead, always the dead with their tables
of multiplication. Both non-epic things
and things other-than took forever.
It was centuries before we could tell you

with any accuracy what a countess was.
History adolesced and kept adolescing
until we could never be sure. Now
someone else does our slaughtering for us
unless we are the ones doing the slaughtering
in which case we are doing it for someones
else. The point was to get home
when what was once home is no longer
yours to return to—just watch
how we give chase, the lunacy of the heart
like a horse in an interminable desert
who catches the scent of water, the point
is so sharp. Everyone got everywhere and still
no one seemed to get anywhere, to arrive
was to begin figuring out that some thing
wasn't quite right and sometimes you were
that something. To sum up: we were there
and we kept licking our hope like it was water
in this desert, so much water we must need
to build a boat. To sum up: we were there
and now we're here. To sum up: The sun
came up, as it often does. Our shadow grew
then disappeared. Yet, somehow, there were
moments of total urgency. We rose to them
like figurative language, we helped
as though we weren't all alone.

& Now

Look at me, I am break-dancing. Next
to a tornado. While doing a stand-up
comedy routine which is made
of my impression of Pauly Shore
doing a stand-up comedy routine.
In front of a mirror. You don't have to
imagine his sadness when the last light bulb
above the mirror gives a snap
and goes dark—you can see it on my face
and this is called teaching composition.
You don't have to remember who he is
to follow my directions.
Somewhere and it is possible
even within walking distance
there is a house. Upstairs
the window is open and that it is
has been forgotten. Look,
there is a fire, you see yourself
in it, you think of how acquiescent
paper is. Look at me, I am Pauly
Shore break-dancing until I can't stand
up. If it were possible to close a book
that were already closed, if it were possible
to double-unread something, that would be
the look looking at me of a Wednesday.
The window wants to close itself
and the animal that is the being open
is nervous. I worry, too, I too worry
and worry. I am holding a watch
in my hand, the watch I am holding
no longer works. Something

is going to happen. I begin a dance
a series of movements it is like
I am laughing. I am reading.
There is breaking. This is not nothing.
And now you are happy.
This is not nothing.

& What Shoulder, & What Art

Sing la la la. Sing huzzah,
huzzah, motherfucker:

The weather's clotted with events
increasingly, the piano you carry

has a piano factory on top of it
and on top of that the city

futzing out in all directions
like a busted hydrant.

The road thins sharply to wire.
But look at the water, glinting

like steel like mirror pepper
in the hard-breathing sunlight.

I have been here before, you think,
the sky full of zippers, the blood

in the trees, don't you feel
like we've been here before—

Five minutes ago, five billion years ago
something realized

there had to be a first step
before a proscenium arch could grin

upon a flautist talking to a fiddle player,
a lover gone down into the earth.

Sing la la la, friend, sing huzzah
like it makes shapes in the dark,

like the dark has to make way
for the shapes that singing takes.

Make-Belief

When I was a child, I could not imagine
not being a cheerleader. At the edge of the road
I stood imagining the components

of a routine. I would celebrate the semi-boiled faces
of the volunteers looking out from the quiet
fire truck, but I was never a child. When I was

never a child, I could not imagine not being
a fire truck. The trees got in the way
of my being a tiny messiah. First, think

of yourself as a tinker toy. Next, never
don't. History was a line I could follow
only follow down a hallway of a stranger's house

in the dark, and History is. Along its track
doors open into closets full of ancient racquets
estranged from the tennis for which they were cut

and strung. You can tell I'm talking about
something else. History is a dotted line, an ellipsis
is a clearing and now we are floating

ladies and gentlemen. Hello Laurie & Ian,
hello all my other friends, tonight the xylophone
sounds like a lilting belt of bones. A door

in this ellipsis History is again and I am no longer
the dream of a cheerleader, no longer contained
like the plastic explosion mimetic in the pom

pom that blooms from my wrist in the fire-forced
drop of sweat on the passing cheek of a volunteer
whose grit quotient got amped as she or he tried

and failed to save the family victrola
from the heedless rampage of accidental flame.
Where was I? Where *wasn't* I. Allow me

to tuck into these masks we float like stunned
kites like last year's pinned-on fashion slivers.
But I am not a cheerleader, I am not a pom

or another pom, or even myself. The split rock
gushes water, the sky sweats manna, how else
to know paradise except already here. History reels

pull backwards. A shout goes up. Whatever
whoever whichever I this is rains ahead like a cloud
with an irrational hope. Another closed door opens,

the closed door of the dead, upon entry of which
more and more and ore and ore. When I was
a spaceship I could not imagine anyone

not wanting to be a docking bay. Same way
when I was a carrot and an ant farm.
This is how we make our way into the day,

when-I-was-a-childing each moment. What comes
after that is knowing better and what comes
after knowing better is knowing you'll never know

better. Let the plastic trees come up,
let the projector booths be giddy with the giddyup
of projecting whatever they may be projecting

and only later we recognize such heartbreaking
and putting-back-together tools, instruments
of suturing light threaded with music

and faces that open the hive of trapdoors
in us. What is this but the compartmentalizing
of infinity, what are we but those compartments?

What can account for the aggressive radiance
of our mortal decorations? When I was a kite,
I was never going to die. When I was a child,

I knew better. But
like I said—

Phil Parma Speaks Over the Body of Philip Seymour Hoffman

PSH (1967–2014)

So much of whatever this is / so much, is letting go
and just listening. Whatever else it is, there's no

silence in it. There's quiet. There's quiet's
constant varieties of noise, of loud—it's

oceanic, an orchestra of need, moments between the decision
speech is, the commitment that is what a noise isn't

only, whether you can help it or not and so much
of whatever is left / is to let everything you hear touch

that listening to your decision, just so.
I don't know, I don't know, no / I know

it sounds / silly / but your ear's really a heart
you see with. It tunes, I mean when you are

truly trying, it tunes to the room, it tunes
to each in the room, how differently they are new

in being stricken, how immediately old hurts rise,
how they are stricken / together, how they recognize

finally and still not believing that whatever this
is / is it. What instruments you have are modest,

except the one: you're a body, and when you're a body
helping another body, when you're a body

having listened as enormously as you can
and then moving with each change, hand or hands

out or down, stepping to the side, kneeling,
running sometimes, trying to anticipate what it feels

like and rush into meeting that feeling,
when you're a body, well—what does anything

do to a body? You're a body that knows
what happens, it's carved in never the same shadow

script / you'll carry the rest of the way—like a tree
shrugs off only being the tree it was, its being

a site of such harm, such trauma, pushing the past toward
a center you can't see till it's later, latest, tree now just boards—

And we're just waiting, just before, on some singing
to soften the waves the sky sends crashing

into the storm doors—. In the rush to the ending
your listening turns into attention turning into attending,

in kind of elegant step with the need in the air,
your heart slows / you're slo-mo, like climbing stairs

into each new interval of help is this the part
is this the part is this the part is this—is any art

even possible here? What's art but an intervention in time
you've already given up, what's help but a nursery rhyme

folded into an impossibly tight space
or horribly free, pilot calling up clouds of flak to ace

until he—I'm sorry, sorry, I never talk this much, I think
this may be the last time, I don't know, I'm breaking

from my lines: The body when you're done
is a little pile. It's a run you leave someone

sad at the end of / and that's if you're lucky / and I know, this
sounds like the part where we turn and kiss

at the tear in the world this one left, and try
to kiss it closed, like our hands could dam up the sky,

but it's the part it is, maybe I'm not even certain
whose lines I'm saying, I'm just eating clock till curtain

but I can't only break, this is the part where I have to say
something. We leave and/or are left, remain, find a way

in what's still here. This is the part where I also know
this is really about me. This is the part where your body sews

me almost up, this is the part where we come to terms,
I can say of you too late what I want, that your turns

left a bruise on the air of how we feel about being ourselves.
Goddamn you, magic savage. Bless your stupid dwelling

in eternity. Mostly what is left by this is not
of this body / but its help: an enlarging, besotted

help / it is so hard / to listen for / so hard—
I stood and waited, but this is not that part.

This is the part where you can be utterly still / and still bow.
And now is the part where I follow you out.

Notes

"A 74-Year-Old Man with Memory Loss and Neuropathy Who Enjoys Alcoholic Beverages"; "The Electric is Excellent in the City"; "Diary of a Busy Doctor"; "Geriatric Anesthesiology"; "Public Health Response to a Rabid Kitten—Four States, 2007"; "Gizmo Idolatry"; and "Marching Band Adjudication Services" all take their titles from a list of titles from the *Journal of the American Medical Association* sent to me in 2008 by Jason Bredle (go here and buy everything twice if you are alive: http://bredlemania.com/work/). I read none of them then and still haven't, but drafted poems for each of the titles in a little over a day. They have since been revised.

"Lester Bangs Talks Scottie"; "Gust Avrakotos Pulls Lancaster Dodd's File in the CIA Archive, 1989"; and "Phil Parma Speaks Over the Body of Philip Seymour Hoffman" form a trilogy of elegies for Philip Seymour Hoffman (1967 – 2014). The speaker in each is a character Hoffman played in a movie. In the first two the speaker considers another character Hoffman played, in the third the speaker considers the late actor himself. The characters—in order of mention—appear in *Almost Famous* (2000), written and directed by Cameron Crowe; *Boogie Nights* (1997), written and directed by Paul Thomas Anderson; *Charlie Wilson's War* (2007), written by Aaron Sorkin and directed by Mike Nichols; and *The Master* (2012), and *Magnolia* (1999), both written and directed by Paul Thomas Anderson.

In 2004, I bought a used copy of Kenneth Koch's *Making Your Own Days*. Tucked inside it, I found a business card for someone whose title was "Grief Recovery Specialist," who worked for an operation called, apparently, Bereavement Company. "Bereavement Company Picnic"; "Bereavement Company Christmas Party"; and "Bereavement Company (0): At the Grief Recovery Academy" are all inspired by this discovery.

"This Song's About a Superhero Named Tony, It's called 'Tony's Theme'" is a misquote of the opening lines of the song "Tony's Theme," off the Pixies' album *Surfer Rosa / Come On, Pilgrim*, released by 4AD in 1988.

"Calming Measures Ahead" is taken from a sign warning cyclists about imminent intentional impediments to the riding of their bicycles.

"At the comestible wedding" is for Amanda Hinnant.

"There are 21 Dogs on the *To Be Destroyed* list" is for Jessica Piazza.

"The Devil is in the Details, God is in the Details, the Devil is God," along with "Electricity is Excellent in the City" was originally accepted for publication in *Copper Nickel* by Jake Adam York. I dedicate both poems to his memory.

"This Will All End in Tarantulas, I Know It" is for Amelia Gray, Mike Krutel, Chris McNeely, and Nick Sturm.

"Voice-Over"; "Fan Mail"; "Fan Mail 2: Nanny Time Approacheth"; "Abridg'd Epic"; and "& Now" were all originally solicited and accepted for publication in *The Offending Adam* by Cody Todd. I dedicate these poems to his memory.

Acknowledgments

Thanks to the editors of the journals and (sometimes now-defunct) internet concerns where earlier versions of these poems first appeared, sometimes with different titles:

Absent: "Some Little Movie." *American Poetry Review:* "Lester Bangs Talks Scottie" and "Gust Avrakotos Pulls Lancaster Dodd's File in the CIA Archive, 1989." *Anti-:* "Public Health Response to Rabid Kitten—Four States, 2007." *Artifice:* "& What Shoulder, & What Art," "Bomb Shelter." *Bennington Review:* "Phil Parma Speaks Over the Body of Philip Seymour Hoffman." *Conduit:* "Good Party," "Gizmo Idolatry." *Copper Nickel:* "The Devil is in the Details, God is in the Details, The Devil is God," "The Electric is Excellent in the City." *Crazyhorse:* "What Isn't Rubble." *Forklift, Ohio:* "Semipro Air Traffic Controller." *Inter/rupture:* "Concept," "After the Film Adaptation of Bobby Gaugin's *Tricycle! Waterfall!*, w/ Off-Brand Orange Juice." *The Laurel Review:* "Staggered Zebra." *Low Rent:* "This Song's About a Superhero Named Tony: It's Called 'Tony's Theme.'" *Matter:* "There are 21 dogs on the *To Be Destroyed* list," "This Will All End in Tarantulas, I Know It," "Available State Compensation Remedies #1: Museum," *Memorious:* "Marching Band Adjudication Services." *The Nepotist:* "Bereavement Company Picnic," "Bereavement Company Christmas Party," "Bereavement Company (0): At the Grief Recovery Academy." *The Offending Adam:* "Voice-Over," "Fan Mail," "Fan Mail 2: Nanny Time Approacheth," "Epic Abrig'd," "& Now." *Rockhurst Review:* "Knit Your Own Sweater, Boss Lady," "Kite Shepherd (2)." *Sixth Finch:* "Kite Shepherd (0)." *Southern Indiana Review:* "Kite Shepherd (1)." *Zocalo Public Square:* "Tracking Shot," "Geriatric Anesthesiology."

Thanks, friends, teachers, torches, torpedoes:
Sarah Barber, Jason Bredle, Jeremy Brightbill, Melissa Broder, Jess Bowers, Will Buck, Scott Cairns, Emily Camp, Stephanie Carpenter, Leah Cheney, Joe Chevalier, Frances Dickey, Katy Didden, Michael Dumanis, Liz Fletcher, Robert Long Foreman, Gabe Fried, Brett Goble, Amelia Gray, Marissa Fugate, Jonathan Hammons, Aaron Harms, Melissa Harms, Matt Hart, Sean Hill, Amanda Hinnant, Jon Knutson, Joanna Luloff, Kate McIntyre, Michael Matthews, Wayne Miller, Speer Morgan, Michael Nye, Chad Parmenter, Molly Pozel, Melissa Range, Todd Richardson, Eve Rifkin, Josh Rivkin, Jeremy Root, Emily Rosko, Tomaž Šalamun, Alex Socarides, Doug Sonnenberg, Jenn Sonnenberg, Nick Sturm, Russel Swensen, Cody Todd, Jamie Warren, Stefanie Wortman, & all the Friend City diaspora, previous and future.

Thanks & then some (family & then some):
Nicky Beer, Murray Farish, Thomas Kane, Jason Koo, Adrian Matejka, Chris McNeely, Dan Rood. Cosgrays, Gwynns, Lopezes, Mysliewics, McKees, Perrins.

Thanks, purveyors of money, employment & support:
University of Missouri

Thank you, Artist:
Amy Freels (amyfreels.com), for better-looking reals.

Thank you, Believer:
Diane Goettel, Black Lawrence Press's madame president, for persisting.

Marc McKee is the author of *What Apocalypse?*, winner of the
2008 New Michigan Press / *DIAGRAM* Chapbook Contest,
and *Fuse* (2011), *Bewilderness* (2014), *Consolationeer* (2017), and
Meta Meta Make-Belief (2019), all from Black Lawrence Press.
His poetry appears widely in online and print journals
such as *American Poetry Review*, *Bennington Review*, *Conduit*, *Copper
Nickel*, *Crazyhorse*, *Forklift, Ohio*, *The Journal*, *Los Angeles Review*,
Memorious, *Sixth Finch*, and several others. He is the managing
editor of the *Missouri Review* and lives in Columbia, Missouri
with his wife Camellia Cosgray and their son, Harold.